Caroline New & Karen Snodin

# Living memory, future worlds:
# Bristol voices on climate change

**Older Women for World Change (OWWCh)**

First published in Bristol, April 2012
by Older Women for World Change

ISBN: 978-1-4716-5645-3 (eBook)
ISBN: 978-1-4716-4614-0 (print edition)

# Bristol and Climate Change

This is the story of how some Bristol women got scared thinking about climate change, and what we did as a result.

In November 2007 the 'Big Event' took place at the Council House, Bristol. This was a day conference about peak oil and climate change and what to do about it, run by Transition Bristol. A group of older women went together, including Caroline and Karen, the authors of this pamphlet.

Fossils fuels (oil, gas, coal) release carbon dioxide into the air when they burn, the first speaker said. Carbon dioxide is a 'greenhouse gas' – it prevents heat escaping into space. Too much greenhouse gas trapping heat in the atmosphere is causing the climate to change. Ice melting in Greenland and Antarctica and extra heat in the oceans is making sea-levels rise.

We got more and more alarmed as we listened. There was nothing sensationalist about the information or the way it was put across. It was matter of fact, and that made it even more frightening.

Carbon trading was in the news in 2007, and one of the speakers talked about why it was bound to fail. The idea behind carbon trading is that rich countries can go on burning huge amounts of fossil fuel if poor countries agree not to. However it's dressed up, that is never going to work.

We went for a cup of tea and a biscuit. It wasn't even mid-morning, and we were looking at the irreversible thinning of the Arctic ice.

The next speaker said that we weren't going to run out of oil anytime soon. That was a relief. But then he said that within a decade, all the oil-producing countries will be producing less and less of the stuff – as happened to Britain's North Sea supply. This would result in a food crisis, since every calory of food we eat takes 10 calories of energy to produce.

It was lunch time. The Council House buzzed. We got some very nice cheese rolls with home made chutney.

Our little group split up. There were workshops going on in other parts of the building. Who can listen to such frightening stuff for long?

We got back together at tea time. Some had listened to a talk on 'Peak Oil meets Climate Change.' Some had been to a workshop on despair. Others were reeling from hearing that our generation – born during the Second World War, or just after it – had used up about half of the world's non-renewable resources.

We remembered times we'd flown to distant countries; how pleased we'd been over the years to be able to buy mangoes and to plug in electric blankets. These luxuries and comforts were all part of what had got human beings into this mess. We worried about what would happen to the children we knew. In a way, our generation had used up their resources.

## Listening to people

The speakers we had heard had been men. Our take was a bit different. We were not scientists or politicians, or even environmental activists. We thought we'd find out what Bristol people were thinking.

On three Saturdays, we went to Broadmead, Clifton Down and Broadwalk in Knowle. In each place we held up a poster saying 'Are you worried about climate change? We'd like to hear.' We didn't argue, we just listened.

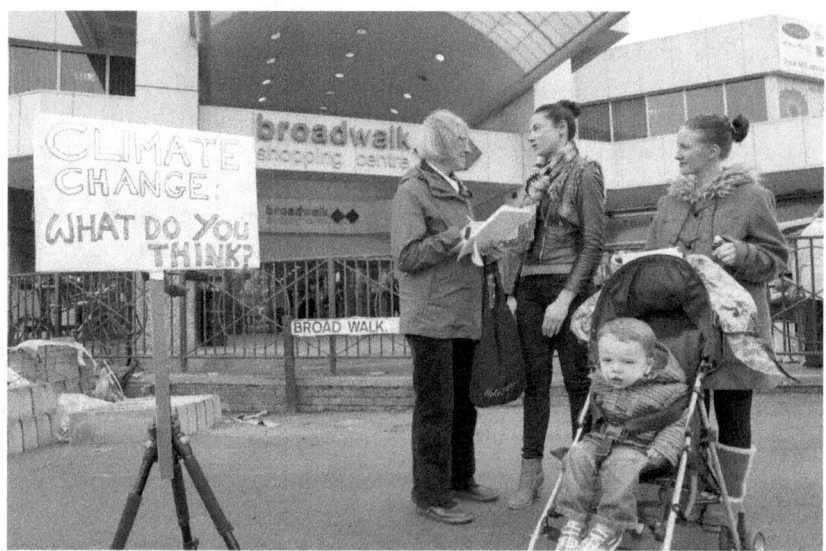

A lot of people talked to us, and most of them felt pretty helpless. Hardly anybody thought the threat was exaggerated, but they didn't like to think about it. A few people thought recycling, or turning off the switches at the plugs, would make everything all right, but most people looked scared or worried. The older ones said, "Well, I'll probably be dead," and the younger ones said, "Nothing we can do about it, is there?"

## Fear...

It's hard to think straight, and take intelligent action, when you are afraid. And anyone who reads the facts about climate change will be afraid. As a result, most of us prefer not to know.

On the other hand, if you can get through the fear long enough to take stock of the situation, and if you then decide what it makes sense to do, you will feel better. You won't be alone with vague fears; you'll be facing a real threat together with many, many others. There's something satisfying in that.

## Bringing it home – Bristol and climate change

It's hard to think on a global scale. So let's think about what is likely to happen to somewhere we know, a place that we love, our home – Bristol.

Exactly what will happen in the future depends upon whatever we all decide to do now. But climate change is already certain – the question is just how bad it will be.

Within 20 - 50 years, everything will change. We'll look at fairly optimistic versions of what mainstream climate scientists are expecting. This is what the children of Bristol who are now five years old are likely to experience by the time they are middle-aged.

- Sea levels will rise. Some parts of the world will be drier, but Britain will experience torrential rainfalls and frequent flooding, making many homeless. The council's contingency plan says the Frome may flood the Floating Harbour, presumably affecting all the Harbourside developments. Tidal flooding is expected to disable the port of Avonmouth as sea levels rise.

- Agriculture everywhere will be in upheaval, leading to food shortages. Farmers in Somerset, Gloucester and Wiltshire will have to adapt to a wetter, warmer climate, with pests previously unknown in Britain and no oil to manufacture pesticides and fertilisers.

- Wars over resources are already happening and will become more frequent and savage. As refugees flee to this country from war, flooding and drought, Bristol will have an even greater problem housing large numbers of people. Urban conflict, terrorism and racism will probably increase.

- Bristol's industries, such as aerospace, engineering, and financial services, are all highly technological and oil-dependent. They will have to adapt or collapse. Cabot Circus and Broadmead will become quieter as the city's commercial life slows down.
- Transport will change as radically as it did when cars displaced horse-drawn carriages. Even 'eco'-cars use too much carbon, and private cars will probably become rare. If it does remain open, not many planes will be using Bristol International Airport.
- Since many modern medicines use oil, we may be forced to rely on preventative medicine and herbal remedies. Energy-greedy hospitals are likely to have less equipment, less medicine and simpler treatments. They will have to become more basic, smaller and locally organised – in complete contrast to what's happening in Bristol right now.

### Are renewables the answer?

Renewables can play a part, but they too have environmental costs. We would need many thousands of windmills around Bristol to satisfy our current needs, for example. Some people think windmills are beautiful, others hate the idea of the Mendips bristling with them. The Severn barrage – so far rejected as a public project – could have given sustainable hydro energy, but its environmental costs have divided public opinion and environmentalists themselves. It's certain that no intelligent decisions can be made on these issues unless we face the reality of the threat from climate change.

### What about nuclear?

Environmentalists are also split on the question of nuclear power. It is clearly dangerous, but the dangers from climate change are so great and immediate that some people think nuclear power is the only way to replace fossil fuels. But even if they are right, there are enormous problems. No one wants to live near a nuclear power station. And the lead-in time to get nuclear power delivering electricity is very long. Let's hope scientists do discover sustainable, harmless forms of energy and practical ways of capturing carbon. But in any case...

We need to use less energy.

### Bristol's carbon dioxide emissions

The greenhouse gases that Bristol adds to the atmosphere every day (6,355 tonnes) would fill a cube the size of Queen's Square. In Bristol, on average, each person adds 5.4 tonnes of carbon dioxide to the atmosphere each year, which is about 15 kg every day. In volume terms, that is 5.5 litres of gas every minute. One day's emissions would fill a cube nearly 2 metres high. 41% of Bristol's emissions comes from industry; 37% from domestic energy use; and 24% from road transport.

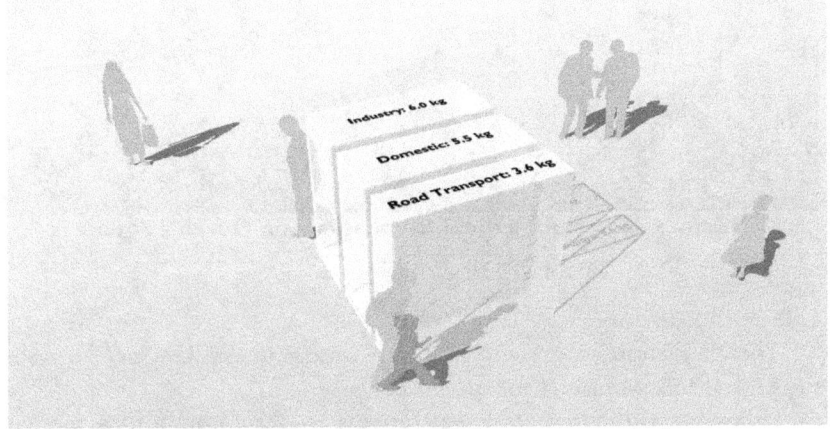

**Bristol's daily per-capita greenhouse gas emissions**
**(actual volume of gas)**

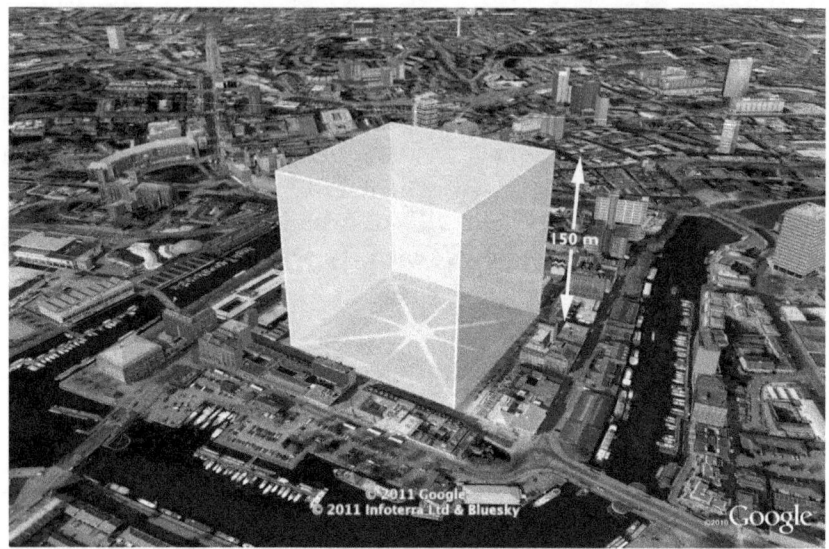

**Bristol's daily carbon dioxide emissions on Queen's Square
(actual volume of gas)**

### Life with less energy

The Transition Movement is about communities taking action – see the end of this pamphlet for more details.

Unless we ordinary people get moving in our communities, we will have no say in policy when governments finally take climate change seriously.

At the moment, our government talks about its commitment to averting climate change, while it puts up rail fares and refuses to tax airlines. But sooner or later the crisis will become so extreme that governments all over the world are forced to take drastic action.

### Don't wait to be pushed

Whichever party is in power, any such top-down action is likely to make poorer people suffer and hardly affect the well-off and rich. That's what's happening in the current recession. It will be harder to impose unfair policies if communities are already organised to use less energy and to improve things for all.

In all our neighbourhoods, we have a valuable resource: citizens who know how you can live with lower carbon emissions – because they've already done it.

As older women, we know from our own experience that a lower-energy future needn't all be depressing. We've experienced losses as well as gains as technology has advanced. In some ways, life might actually improve. Communities could become stronger and more supportive again, for instance.

The Bristol people we have interviewed for this pamphlet and exhibition can all remember less energy-extravagant times. Many of their memories are happy.

In the next section you can read our interviews. We think they hold clues to a better future.

# Anne

Anne lives in Stockwood with her husband Pete, in a house with a big garden where they grow vegetables. They don't have a car.

## "We never threw anything out."

I grew up with my parents and two younger brothers. My father was an electrician, and my mother did various jobs to bring in a bit of money.

My school and the shops and parks we used were close together. We knew all the shop-keepers. We used to go to different shops for different things, and often we would queue up at each shop. Shopping took quite a time because people constantly stopped to chat, but it wasn't as stressful as nowadays, because there were fewer choices to be made. Milk was delivered to our door, a man came round pulling a mobile trailer with bread, and there was a mobile grocery shop and a mobile fishmonger.

Buses were always there when you wanted them. We walked a lot, and we all had bikes. We used to go for family bike rides into the country at weekends. One of my favourite times was blackberrying. We would go by train, four stations up the line, and then walk across the fields.

### A strong sense of community

I remember a strong sense of community. Everybody knew each other and we went to each other's birthday parties

We were never hungry. My mother could make something from nothing. We never threw food away. We kept chickens that ate all the left-overs. My father knocked up the chicken run himself, and we got plenty of eggs.

### The kitchen was always warm

We had four rooms downstairs, but the only heating was a coal fire in one of them. The kitchen was always warm because of the cooking. There was no heating upstairs. When my grandmother came to live with us, she had a fire in her room – I remember her carrying a shovel of burning coals from the living room fire to her room. It didn't matter too much if she dropped the odd burning coal because we didn't have carpet on any of the floors.

We had a wonderful time in the winter of 1947, skating on the frozen pavements. I do remember sometimes having painful frozen hands.

## Washing clothes was a huge performance

The whole kitchen was filled with steam. We had a big copper for whites (all the towels and sheets), which we washed with "blue bags". All clothes were made from natural fibres, so they took a long time to dry. We had a rack in the kitchen and a mangle to help with drying.

We never threw anything out. Not only clothes, everything was repaired: radios, bikes - we never threw anything out. We turned sheets sides to middle.

## We had a lot more freedom than children today

We went to the parks on our own, and when I was eight, I often took my baby brother to the playground. We played out in the road because there was hardly any traffic.

We didn't have many books, but we had comics every week: Beano, Dandy and Eagle. I had dolls. One Christmas my present was one of my own dolls that my mother had mended in the dolls' hospital - I was very pleased.

Birthdays were big occasions: everyone came to my parties. I didn't get many presents, but no one did. I remember getting a mac and hat for my fifth birthday.

## I could cope with less energy use

We are all more comfortable now, but we've lost a lot. Nobody knows how to make curtains, knit or make rag rugs. I think we could all live very comfortably without so much waste.

# Gordon and Barbara

Gordon and Barbara are both South Bristolians,. His father was a tannery clerk and hers a telephone engineer. They met through Scouts and Guides and got married in the 1950s. They brought up two children, while Gordon worked with the electricity generating board and Barbara as a medical secretary. Since retiring, Gordon has become a local historian and until recently a Blue Badge guide.

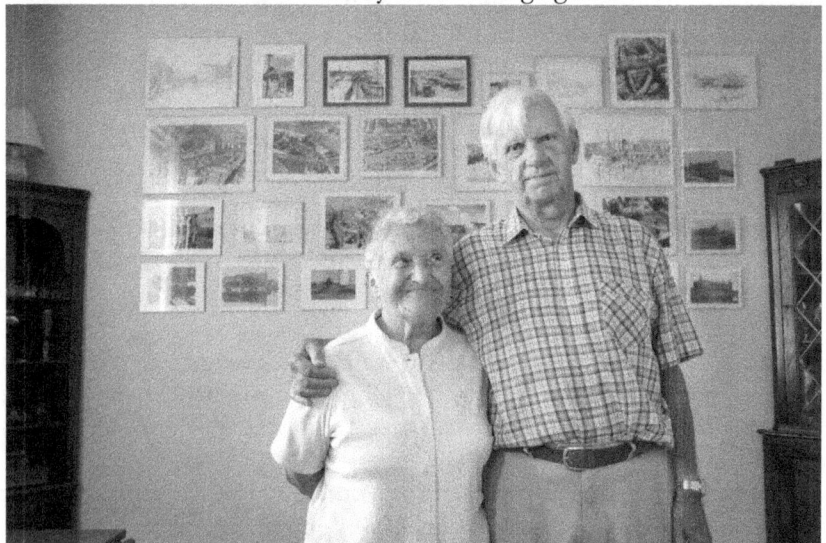

## "You didn't have to have things"

### We were never bored

Gordon: We went to youth club twice a week, we loved amateur dramatics. There was no need for booze to have a good time on a Saturday night.

Barbara: Life was more local. Every street had a corner shop, grocer's, butcher's. You didn't have to remember what you wanted, you could just go and get it.

Gordon: Mr Bridle the farmer used to come with his horse and cart – I can still see the horse now – his fruit and veg was probably picked that same day on his farm in Long Ashton.

Barbara: Food was seasonal then, so it was fresh. You didn't have tasteless Spanish strawberries. You might buy a crate of apples – Coxes would last for weeks.

Gordon: No worry about sell by and use by dates. If you were hungry, you ate it.

## You knew your neighbours

Gordon: You might not get on with them but you knew them and it was pretty true that doors were left unlocked. During the war you were pushed together even more because of fire rotas and so on.

## You didn't have to have things

Barbara: When I was a child, I didn't have any school shorts for PE. The teacher said 'See if any of your fathers have old trousers.' She made me some smashing shorts. These days you'd be ashamed. In those days you didn't have the feeling that you had to have things to be in with others.

Gordon: There were three lads in my class with hobnailed boots. Much later I realised they got them from the council. But no one thought the worse of them for that. There wasn't the competition about clothes that comes from advertising. Another thing: nowadays they don't produce things which are capable of being repaired. Even if you do get hold of the materials no one knows how to do it. There is no financial incentive to mend things.

## Our energy use was minimal

Barbara: We only heated one room. We used to undress by the fire then run upstairs.

Gordon: It was a big deal if there were visitors and you lit a fire in the front room. Mostly our energy use was minimal. My grandfather had a big stone hot water bottle to put in his bed an hour before he went up. We were too young to bother.

Barbara: We had a geyser in the bathroom and we heated water for washing up in the kettle. We had gas boilers for doing the washing. On a Monday night after work at half past five I used to put it on and by 8 pm I'd have done the washing. Then I'd go out the back to use the mangle – we had one that folded down into a table - very modern! In the late 50s we got a twin tub – my God! Gordon was out at night school till nine. By the time he came home I'd have done the washing.

### It was a different mind set

Gordon: Before the war we never borrowed money. Then Dad paid a deposit on a vacuum cleaner. That was the first time. It was a different mind set...

# Pam

Nowadays, Pam lives in an old people's home in Clifton. Her father had been a chief instructor in the military, and after he died the family's standard of living fell and they moved to a village near Salisbury. When she grew up, Pam became a medical secretary. She has vivid memories of wartime – both of closeness and deprivation.

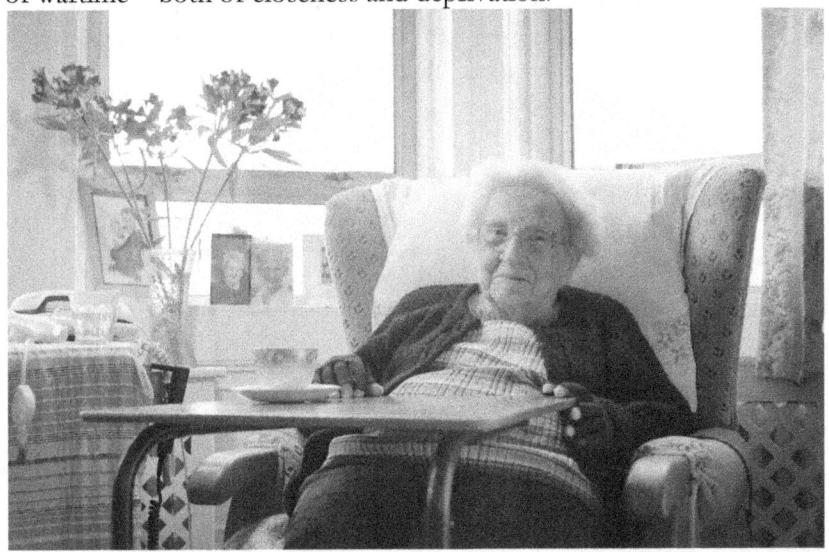

## "During the war people were much more helpful than normal. You felt you were lucky to be where you were and alive"

There was a lovely friendly shop in the village. It sold everything from spades to lemonade. But they listened in to all your telephone calls. When you went into the Post Office, they would say 'We hear you're thinking of moving!'

### We grew a lot of our food

We even used to sell a lot of raspberries and strawberries. We kept all the left overs. If we didn't eat them our two dogs did.

It was fun cycling around the countryside. We used to put our bikes on a train, stay over night in a youth hostel in the Cotswolds. That was enjoyable.

During the war parties were always planned for moonlit evenings, because of the blackout. We would dance, and the hostess would provide whatever she could in the way of eats. There was much more camaraderie and helpfulness than today.

I hated mending. Once we were on rationing, you had to do it.

And the food was boring. But during the war, you felt you were lucky to be where you were and alive.

It's so convenient today.

# Margaret

Margaret was born in 1940, youngest of 7 children, 6 of them girls. She lived in a big house in Totterdown as a child. She has a huge extended family, many of Irish heritage. She now lives with her husband in a council flat in Redcliffe.

## "I used to say, 'Oh yes we gotta have that!'"

Our Dad used to walk from Portishead to Wiltshire. That was to see our mother, she was looking after her parents who were ill in West Lavington. Dad walked along the railway track – because he was a stoker. It's all the more amazing when you think that he was gassed in the First World War so he had bad lungs.

### We had a tin bath

We used to boil the water for it in a bucket on the stove, and we'd take turns having a bath in front of the fire. As a teenager I used to wait till I knew everyone was out except our mum.

When we went to bed, we had candles. We had coal fires in the bedrooms, and we lit them before we went to bed then let them die down. I shared a bed with two of my sisters. We used to have fun, mind. They used to chat chat chat. I used to say, "Stop chatting, shut up, I want to sleep".

### I got a job in Wills cigar factory in 1955

My job was to make the cigars and pack them. I stayed there till I got married, then I had to give in my notice, and reapply for my own job. I left again when I had our Sue.

When I got married, I wanted a new life. I got married in 1962, but I lived with my mother till 1965. The house was condemned, there were buckets everywhere catching the drips.

We moved to Proctor House and there was central heating and hot water. We still only bathed once a week, because you got some money back if you didn't use too much hot water. Then they put in meters, and the bills went sky high... Gas was cheaper, we used it for cooking. We didn't cook every day, I used to go to the fish shop.

### I wanted new things

When I was young the clothes were passed down for the girls, and my Mum knitted. I got some new baby clothes for Sue, though I did get given a lot. I had a new pram. I used to say, "Oh yes, we gotta have that cos we're better than she!"

We mended everything when we were little. I used to darn. I used to sew. I was never good at it, but I used to do it. It's so convenient today, you just don't want to mend things!

# George

George came to Britain in 1961, from Portland in Jamaica. He used to work at St Anne's Board Mill making paper. In his fifty years in the UK, he has only been out of work for 11 months, and he's still working as part-time caretaker at St Werburgh's Community Centre. He celebrated his eightieth birthday there recently with a big party of family and friends.

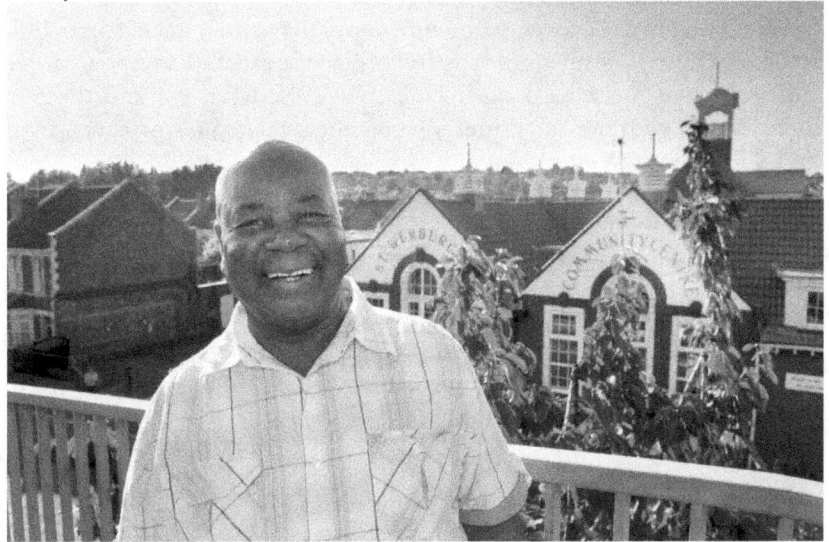

## "You should help and preserve things for your children and your children's children"

I was born in the West Indies and I lived there during the war. I was just a boy at school. We didn't have electricity, we used paraffin in Tilley lamps. When we couldn't get kerosene in those days we used coconut oil: it smelt nice. We raised pigs and goats, and we had our little gardens – we did a lot of cultivating at that time.

As children we never felt it so hard. We had plenty of local food like bananas. We didn't have much money or anything but we were happy – we had something to eat and clothes to wear. It's only when you see the next person who's got more that you get a bit jealous. I was used to a quiet life in the country.

21

I came to England in 1961. Coming from the West Indies I wasn't looking for a hundred percent, but my friend said 'You'll do better here.' It wasn't all easy. Training and things a person could get would pass you by. They would give the leaflets to other people, not to me. When they were giving out the work clothes everyone else would get the better ones, that sort of thing. But I'm not a person to complain, I made a good life here.

### I don't like to see waste

We don't waste food. Sometimes you have to chuck some little thing away, when your tummy is full – but not much. I'm not a waster. That's part of my caretaking. I hate to see the lights on and the fans going round with no one there, wasting energy, like no one cares. I will go to any length to stop that.

### I could cut down a little

As for using less energy in the future, I could manage that. I make my own clothes. I'm always fixing and fixing. I'm used to a worse life. I believe in God anyway. You should help and preserve and look after things for your children, and your children's children, and their children, but I find it hard to believe God would let it all be destroyed.

# Joyce

Joyce lives in Knowle where she was born in 1921, the middle of three sisters. She went to primary school in Totterdown, and got a scholarship to Colston's Girls' School. Her father was an accountant and she went on to art college, and for much of her life was a book illustrator (she still does exquisite drawings). During the war her job was to write letters of commiseration to the families of Canadian soldiers killed in the fighting. Every letter had to be different.

## "The first thing I think about is the corner shop."

Here you bought dolls, groceries, beads, soaps, coal, and bread. I remember my grandma's huge red and green mangle, squawky from the wooden rollers – and sheets and pillow-cases and steam all over the kitchen, and Grandma in a large flowery apron.

In the summer we had a trip to Weston. We climbed a little ladder to get into the Charabanc. We would sit all high-and-mighty on the plank-like seats and feel quite superior!

### I remember having measles

I was put in my mother's bed and they lit a small fire every night, which made the room far too hot. I had a small teddy bear, and after I got better I couldn't find it. I was upset when my mother told me they had burnt it, in case it was infected.

People became frightened when they heard there was diphtheria about. I remember Mum keeping us off school when a little girl died in the next road from ours. Scarlet fever, measles, polio – all these were horrible. There was a small hospital near Dundry, and in the summer it became full of patients. We all hung a blanket soaked in Jeyes Fluid over the door. Who knew whether this did any good – who can tell?

### In the twenties, electric lights began to appear in posh places

We had gas lamps at home. We knelt on the window seats every evening, waiting for the old lamplighter; with his pole and heavy boots, climbing up the hill. He sang the same song every day "Keep the lamplight burning, 'til the boys come home." It made me cry.

It was my job to change the flypapers. One in the dining room and two in the kitchen – I had to change them every day. It was a revolting job! There were no refrigerators, but then a net cage was fitted outside the kitchen wall to keep the meat fly-proof. Ma was very proud. Eventually we moved to a larger house, with a bath.

Milk came in large churns, beautifully clean. The milkman's horse obligingly dropped a bucketful of garden manure, and my mother used to make me collect it while she kept the front door shut.

# Mary

Mary was born in 1925. For many years she and her husband Tom were well known Bristol activists. Now Mary is living in a residential home in Clifton.

## "The best thing about my childhood was the freedom."

Children had much more freedom then than they do now. We went for miles and miles, on foot and bike, on the trams and buses – anywhere as long as we had a friend with us.

We never travelled far as a family. We had a car at one point, but my father never learnt to drive, and my mother was terrified of the Great West Road. My grandmother used to pay for us to have a holiday on the Isle of Wight, and we went by train. When the war came we sold the car.

My father had a steady job. He was an insurance salesman, so we were never short of money, but we were pretty economical about everything. Everything that could be mended, was, and there was always a big pile of mending waiting.

### My mother was good at making do

She worked hard to make ends meet, especially during the war. She preserved eggs in isinglass, and salted beans for the winter. We were very conscious of waste. We weren't allowed to leave food and if we were hungry after a meal we were told to eat bread.

I don't remember being cold before the war. The kitchen was kept warm by the back boiler and we spent a lot of our time there. But we were evacuated to a very cold house in 1940 and we had to sleep in our clothes.

### Some things were hard

School was terrifying. There was a general fear of authority. The teachers were so strict and you were always punished for stepping out of line. Then I was always afraid that my parents might die – I don't think people are as conscious of death today.

People's imaginations are more limited now. Books were more important then, and time was less pressured, and there were no computers and television.

There was a sense of fairness, at least during the war, that we've lost now. Nobody liked rationing but it meant no one went hungry – actually children were healthier – and we were all in the same boat. There weren't the consumer pressures there are today, not as much keeping up with the Jones.

# Nazmah and Gouri

Nazmah and Gouri belong to a South Asian Women's group at Barton Hill settlement. They live in East Bristol, and both have experience of living lower carbon life styles in their countries of origin. Nazmah was born in Mauritius and Gouri in South India.

## Nazmah

# "I miss the old fashioned stuff"

When I was quite small we had paraffin lamps. Cooking was with wood-burning stoves in the open air in a kitchen built outside because mum didn't like the smoke and the smells. The dining room was right next to it.

We all thought modernisation was a very good thing. As soon as electricity came in (some time in the 50s) my dad modernised the kitchen. We got an electric iron, a TV and so on. We were going up in the world!

My dad had started to make lots of money and he thought because we were young women we needed things to look better. My mum had suffered so much. She married when she was very young. Before that, she'd been used to good stuff, but when she went to live with her parents-in-law things were lacking. She was really happy when dad could afford to modernise. Now, I miss the old fashioned stuff.

We didn't need heating, what we needed was ventilation. The doors had been open all of the time. Then, when we became modernised, the doors were closed.

Our family grew most of our food. My grandfather had fields and a market garden. We ate our own fresh produce. No pesticides. My uncle had a farm and gave us meat and milk.

Coming to the UK was a shock. We landed during the day, but it was November and so dark, that it could have been night time. The houses in London were so small and terraced. Then I became a nurse, and I moved to Surrey, which I liked better. I still miss the sunshine. I lost the normal contact with my family. But I have adapted.

Back home, there wasn't much waste. We bought everything for the day. Fish was straight from the sea. When I came here and saw things in the freezer and the supermarket I thought "What's all this? I can't believe it!" I looked everywhere for fresh food.

In England, everything is provided. I've got used to it too. We need to be told how to be energy efficient, how to cut down on wastage – though I've done that all my life to save money. I've always told my family – "If you waste, you'll have to pay!"

**Gouri**

# "Here, people use too much energy"

I was brought up in a village in South India. We had no tap and no running water, just a well. My dad was a teacher with 12 children. He taught himself carpentry. My parents had a big house. We only had to buy lamb because we had cows and hens and buffalo, which also gave us milk.

This is how I came to England.

When we were teenagers (six sisters and one brother) my father sold up and the whole family went to live in the city of Poona, where we only had one room. My mum worked as a nurse, my father as a carpenter, and my brother in a bus factory.

I went to school, then to college. I wanted to go to university, but there was no money so I became a midwife and health visitor and learnt family planning.

After a year I became engaged and in 1970 I came to the UK. We didn't meet till we married. I had to leave my family. I was very sad, but that's life.

Here, people use too much energy. They spend a lot, they don't care. I am very good with it. We don't waste anything.

## Sabaa and Faaduma

Sabaa and Faaduma were refugees from the civil war in Somalia, who now live in Redcliffe with their families. Although they refer to waste of food, Somalia has always used very little of the world's energy. Sabaa was an accountant in Somalia and is now a cleaner. In Somalia, Faaduma was training to be a judge. She is now a learning support worker. They are respectively secretary and chair of the local Somali Women's Group.

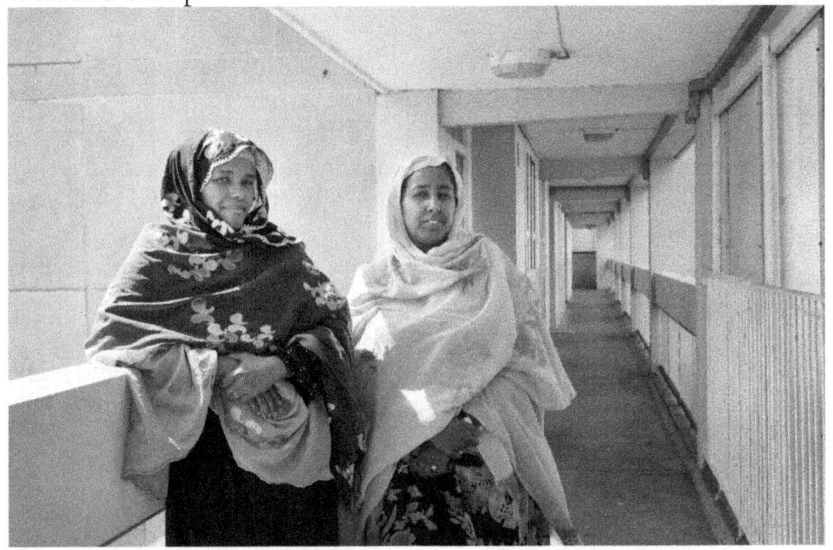

## "If I have to save energy here, I could do without the microwave, the kettle and the toaster, which I never had in Somalia."

In Somalia we often throw stuff away because it isn't fresh.

Sabaa: Some people waste more than here. In Somalia we are not used to fridges. Every day we would take a basket and go to the market.

Faaduma: My mother cannot bear the way we eat meat here which has been in the fridge a long time. She thinks it can't be fresh. In the countryside, where there are no fridges, no electricity, you eat meat soon after it has been killed. In the city, even if you had a fridge, you would buy your food fresh from a shop every day.

I've noticed that when English people have parties they are more exact about amounts. I think we throw away a lot of food that is good into the bin.

In Somalia, because of the climate, we didn't need heaters and hot water. We didn't have microwaves and electric cookers. We didn't spend so long in the kitchen as we do here. If I have to save energy here, I could do without the microwave, the kettle and the toaster, which I never had in Somalia.

'

Sabaa: In our religion you are not allowed to eat a lot when your neighbour doesn't have enough to eat.

Beggars come round after meals – they know when you've had breakfast and they come and sing outside the house hoping you will give them the leftovers. Sometimes they sing about how you will go to Paradise, if you give them food.

Faaduma: The problem here is that we never know who is in need and who is not.

# Harry

Harry is a member of Bristol's Jewish community. He moved here over forty years ago, so his children are Bristolians. He works in financial services.

## "Climate change? I don't have a clue what we can do"

As children, we would play in the bomb-damaged houses in our street, and collect the shrapnel. One day our school was closed. It had been hit by an incendiary bomb.

### We didn't know what we were missing

I went into the RAF in 1953 at the age of 18 – National Service. It was 4 shillings (20p) a day, 28 shillings (£1.40) a week. The eight weeks basic training was known as "square bashing" because of the hours of drill. We were instructed how to use and clean a rifle and other weapons. The idea was to convert us into soldiers, sailors or airmen. I remember rationing with points for food, and coupons for clothes and furniture. We didn't notice anything bad about it, because it was what it was. We were allocated a maximum of four ounces of sweets a week – so what? Bananas, we never saw them, did it matter? Not really. We'd never heard of them, probably, so we didn't know what we were missing.

### There were two power points when we moved in

When I got married in 1960 the first house we bought was a pre-war semi, no central heating, and a coke boiler in the kitchen. The plumber put a couple of pipes off the kitchen boiler and we had a radiator in the hall. We thought this was luxury. Did we have carpet? No, of course we didn't. We had lino. There were two power points when we moved in. A 5 amp one in the kitchen, and one on the landing. By the time we got married we had thirteen power sockets. We did the work ourselves and Southern Electric came along and checked them.

There were two other couples, married about the same time as ourselves, we would go round to each others houses on a Saturday evening and have coffee and play cards or something. We'd go and help each other out, with say, decorating or tiling bathrooms, I'm quite good at that. Very much do-it-yourself.

We were quite excited when we got our first television, and we were very excited when we got this old banger of a car. The first fridge we had was a second hand gas fridge, early on in married life. My wife was working, earning five pounds a week, six days a week in a hardware store.

**Climate change? I don't have a clue what we can do**

If you have a piece of equipment and it breaks down you don't bother to replace it because it's cheaper to throw it away and start again. You could almost fly to London for the price of a train ticket. Is this sensible? No.

You've got far more choice today. I object to going into a supermarket and seeing all this fruit from Peru, strawberries from America. It's ridiculous. What's wrong with things grown in England?

# Parveen

Parveen was born in Pakistan and came to the UK as a young mother with her first child. She is now a widow with four children, three of whom have left home. She works for Dhekbal in Barton Hill settlement, which runs an Asian elderly-sitting service.

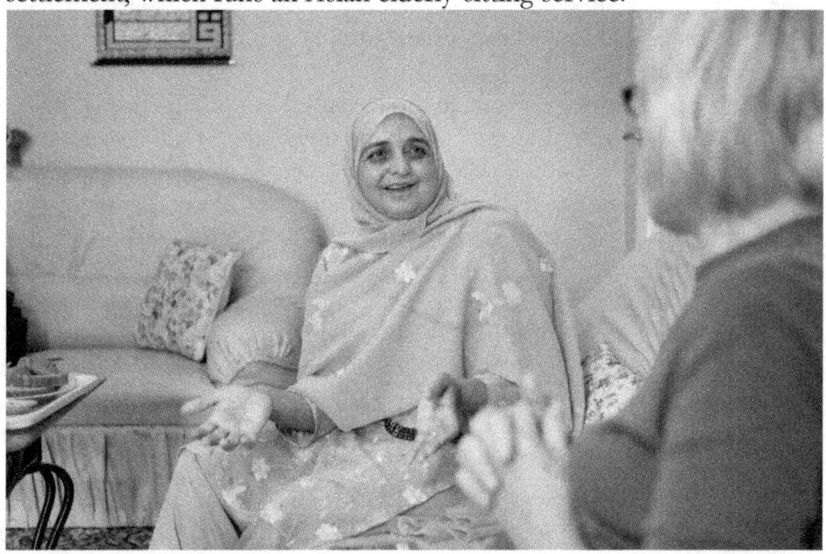

## "You don't need so many things around you"

Fifty years ago, we had no electricity in our village in Pakistan. We used to have an oil lamp in each room. When I was in school I used to keep one next to me, because they were bright enough for the house, but not really to study by.

**The houses were made of mud bricks in those days.**

They were low houses and they stayed cold. In the summer we never said "Oh it's too hot", like people do now. We didn't need air conditioning. We had one kitchen outside, and one inside in case it rained. When I was little we burned wood, then we got an oil stove.

I was eighteen when my parents got a generator. Before that, we never felt we needed it. At night we used to sleep on the roofs. There were steps up to the roofs, and the houses were joined together. We used to chat to each other - that was really nice, but it doesn't happen any more.

There was a garden outside the house, at a little distance, where all the neighbours used to go in the heat of the day. It had a spring and a well that was covered over. You could have a shower there, we used to take food, there were small beds so you could sleep, and we used to spend half a day there. There was one part that was just for women. Now the wells have all been destroyed. There are just big pumps for irrigating the fields.

When the electricity came, people started spending more time in their houses because they had fans and light, they could sleep there when it was hot, so slowly slowly the custom of going to the garden faded away. Nowadays during the summer after noon, people are all inside, and the doors are closed. It's completely Westernised.

**Now Pakistan is just like here**

When I first came to this country, when I went back to Pakistan I felt really at home, because it was so different. Now, when we go, it's just like here! It's nicer than here, actually, because my parents have en suite bedrooms, but there's no enjoyment any more. There's air conditioning, and the kitchen is indoors just like here.

In some villages things are just the same as before and people are fine, they survive. I don't think if you ask them they will say "Oh, we miss electricity". Everybody wishes for things. But when we do have those things, we think back, and then we realise what we have lost. In those times people worked hard but they were more loving to each other, there was community.

**I do worry about climate change.**

Floods, earthquakes, all these happenings are because of that. I remember a few years ago when we went home we went to see a place where they used to have ice mountains. Water was flowing from them very fast, and they told us they had never melted before.

I don't think I will mind using less energy. You don't need so many things around you. You need one light, a fridge, but not two or three lap tops, a computer, TV in your bedroom. You do need a car for some things, but personally I would rather not use the car.

It's true that, living here, a part of my mind is always in Pakistan, especially because my parents are there. But we always have telephones, that's one of the good things. If I had to choose, I would have telephones.

# David

David and his wife Sarah moved to Bristol in the 1970s. They live in St Andrews. David had fifteen minutes of fame recently when he chained himself to a historic lamppost to protest its being moved to Clifton. He studies local history and helped get a memorial in the park to those who risked their lives to save the crew of a Wellington bomber that crashed there in 1941. He's also starred in a TV programme about allotments.

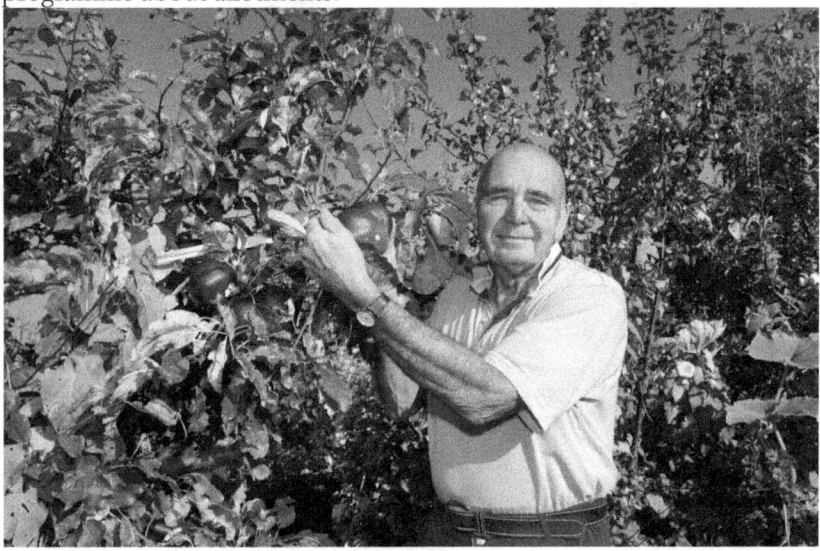

## "Sitting round the coal fire being baked in the front and frozen at the back, and ice on the inside of the windows. That was life"

From the age of six I lived in a very tiny agricultural bungalow in Northamptonshire. I have memories of sitting round the coal fire being baked in the front and frozen at the back, going to bed with a stone hot water bottle in a sock, and ice on the inside of the windows.

That was life. We had a well, but it was contaminated... People chucked their sewage onto the gardens and it seeped into the water supply so we had to have water delivered in a tank.

Before we had the range taken out, you could open the oven door and put your feet in the oven. I was always being told that I would get chilblains, but I never seemed to get them. You put clothes on to keep warm and you took them off to cool off.

I remember us getting a fridge. We had a pantry before. Then we had an electric boiler in a shed across the yard, and my mother used to hand wash in there. I remember the blue bags, you used to put it on you if you got a sting. Mum did her brothers' washing, since they were both bachelors. Eventually she got a twin tub, but she still had to dry the clothes. I've got lots of memories of steaming clothes around the fire.

Till I left home we never had hot running water. You used a kettle and washed in the sink. The bathroom was an outhouse. At least we had an inside loo. Every so often, Christmas, Easter or holidays, we would boil up some water and carrry it across the yard and pour it into a bath. Of course everybody had to use it, and last one in was my mother.

We had a garage on the side, and quite a nice garden. My father wasn't a great food grower. We had apples, a few veg. Other people up the road had pigs and all sorts. The people next door had chickens. In the country, food was quite cheap.

**I played out all the time**

The nearest house, except for the terrace, was seven and a half miles away. There was an old American airbase about four miles away. It was great to go there and peep through the wire and get chased away. I spent all my time out, climbing trees, mushrooming.

We would all play football in the street – the cry would go up 'police!' and the policeman would come ambling along on his bike, and we'd all hide in the ditch till he'd gone. Very few cars, safe for bikes.

**The worst thing was poverty**

There were constant arguments about money. I got a pair of long flannel trousers. I was coming home from school on my bike and I ran into the back of a car and ripped the knees of these trousers. I was sobbing my heart out, and everyone thought it was because I was hurt, but it wasn't. It was because I knew my trousers would have to be darned.

## I cannot bear to see things chucked away

I go to the car boot sale every week if I can. I sometimes buy things and sell them, for fun, then I use that money to buy things I want. Sometimes it goes wrong, sometimes it's a fantastic bargain. We brought our pregnant daughter's buggy for £40, it even has a temperature control. £400 new. It upsets me to go down the recycling centre and see the amount of stuff that is thrown away. Great lengths of timber, going into landfill.

Some people's junk is what someone else needs. If I put stuff on the wall out there, nine times out of ten it's gone by the end of the day. I had an old fashioned drill stand, I never used it so I finally got rid of it, then Ben my son wanted it, and I was very apologetic but I got one in the car boot for a pound, solid metal, not a bit of plastic on it anywhere, it must have cost £18 or £19.

We compost all our kitchen waste for the garden and the allotment. We recycle all our paper and cardboard. Sometimes after two weeks we've only got one small bag of rubbish.

I think those people whom we'd see as irresponsible because they don't recycle are alienated from the community. It's to do with feeling connected to things around you. You've got to bring them back in to feel part of it, that's all you can do.

# Betty and Di

Betty was born in 1925 and her daughter Di in 1951. Betty worked as a guard on the railways during the war, then in John Hall's paint factory. Until recently, Di worked as a local administrator for the Transport and General Workers' Union. The family have lived in Hotwells, Knowle West, Hartcliffe and Redcliffe.

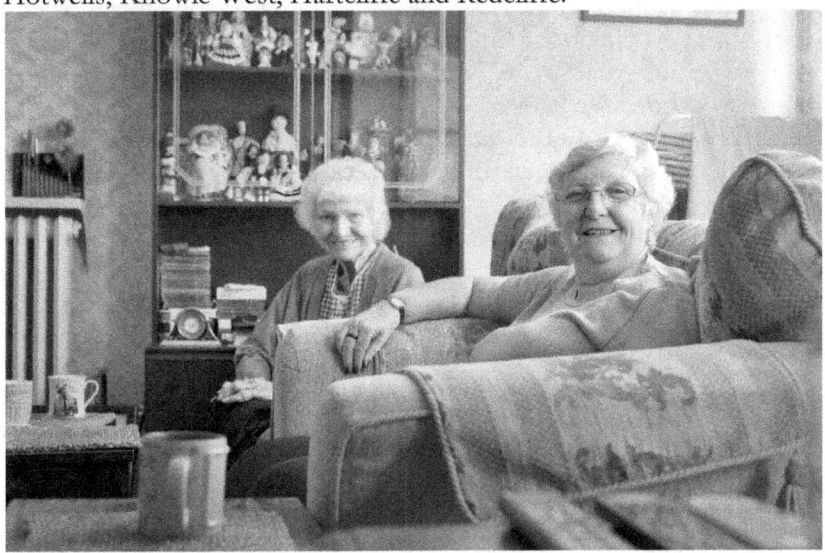

## "I thought electricity was so exciting. I kept switching it on and off"

Betty: The fuel we used to have was coke, because it was cheaper than coal. We had gas lighting in some of the rooms, but candles to take us to bed.

We had good parents, didn't us. My mother died when I was a baby, and a couple of years later my dad married again, but I couldn't have had a better step mother.

Course, my dad was out of work for years. He worked for Dysons, when I was a little girl, then he came home and said 'I've got the sack'. I thought he meant he had something nice in a sack, like Father Christmas, but he said 'No, no no, not that sort of sack.'

Anything he was offered, he did, otherwise we wouldn't have had any money at all. But they were only little jobs. Every Christmas he worked for the Post Office. We were poor. But then, everyone in the district was poor.

My dad didn't believe in hitting children. That was unusual. He was very left wing, but he was ever so popular. Up until a couple of years ago old people would be telling me how much they liked him. He had a great sense of humour as well. I have a bit of a tear sometimes, when I think about my childhood, how lucky I was, in a way.

I was in hospital, mind, with TB, when I was seven. Frenchay it was. It was horrible. It really was. My Dad found out what was going on and he took me away from there. They used to shove us out on the verandah, whatever the weather was like, apart from if it was actually raining or snowing.

I've gotta laugh, because my Dad said to the doctor, "I don't like how she's treated here. She's even hit by one of the nurses. I'm going to take her away." And the doctor said, "If you do, and she dies, I'll have you for manslaughter". (Laughs)

We lived in St Georges Rd, next door to the Three Tuns. I couldn't go to school, they took me to clinics down by College Green, I had to have X-rays. But the teacher used to send books and things so I kept up with my education.

Di: That was the big change, when the family was moved from a slum to council housing, with a bathroom and everything. Mum and Dad were still living with Mum's parents for a couple of years, then they come up to the Hartcliffe estate, which was mud at the time.

## It was lovely in terms of neighbourliness

Our next door neighbours became our very close friends, and people down the street. We used to have barbies before people had barbies – no equipment. We used to cook stuff inside and bring it out, get the music.

Betty: Once we moved into the council house, we had electric light. I thought it was so exciting. I kept switching it on and off, my dad went mad. He said 'You can't do that, we've got to pay for it!

Di: We had coal fires with guards, didn't have heating properly in the rest of the house, we never had electric fires or paraffin heaters, just one room and hot water bottles, not very different from when you were little, Mum. But we had gas fires put in later.

Betty: And another thing, fridges.

Di: All these changes made life easier for the woman. It was real drudgery if you had to wash everything by hand, wring everything out, and beat your carpet instead of just going round with a vacuum cleaner. Technology meant you could do a lot more with your life.

Betty: We never wasted anything. I'm still funny about that now. Course, I worked for Oxfam for 11 years, in the Bedminster shop. If I saw any waste, I used to get funny about it.

Di: They're wasting stuff now. That community room down there gets used as a dumping ground. When I go down to clear it out, there's children's things that are in perfect condition, even a girl's bike. Some of it we actually used but I took the rest to the charity shop up the road. It's out of date, that's why it is, it's not the modern thing. One thing chucked out was an old fashioned television, it's a lovely screen but it's only a little screen.

I think people are greedy now. They've got things we never even dreamed of. But I don't think it does them any good.

# University of Withywood

The University of Withywood is a discussion and action group of local people that meet in Anton Bantock's Withywood bungalow (www.universityofwithywood.org.uk) We talked to Sue, Don, Heather, Annie and Anton.

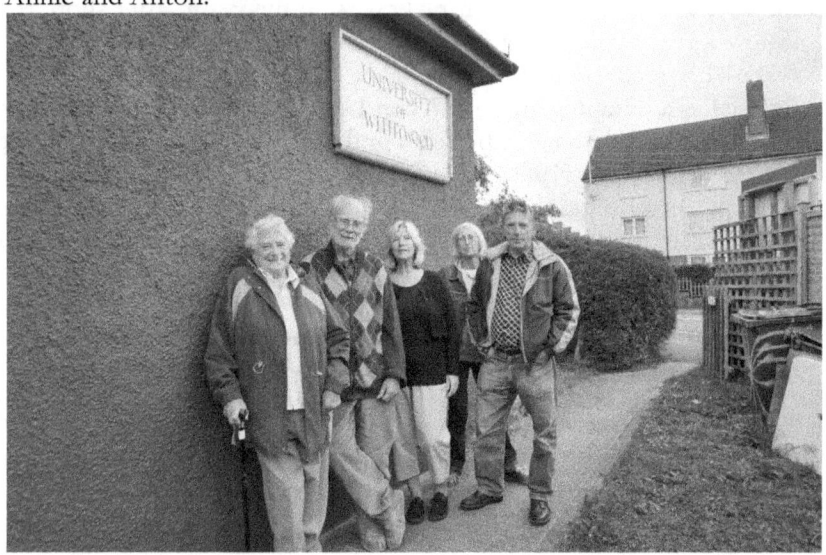

## "We'll be forced back to the old ways"

Anton: It's only recently that we've had any heating: we've had to get through the winter in a bungalow with no central heating and no cavity walls. We keep moving.

Sue: It brought back my childhood...

Don: Going with carts to the Bowery to get coke for the fire.

Annie: You used to see an old woman with a pram full of coal.

Heather: My mother used to make rag rugs, and when it was cold you put them on the beds.

Sue: We were glad our grandparents lived with us because they had long overcoats, and we used to put them on the beds at night.

I lost my Nan when I was 15 to Coronation Street.

That was the worst thing that happened to me. I used to be able to go round and get a spoonful of malt and cod liver oil shoved in my mouth as soon as I went in the door. "Open your mouth!" But then we could talk for hours. But as soon as they had a TV, Coronation Street gripped her. From then on I only saw her back.

## The entertainment was good

Annie: We didn't have television, we had radio. My first one was a piece of board with instruments on and you had to have an accumulator to be charged by someone down the road who was better off than you were.

Don: I liked the Saturday morning pictures, the serials. I used to go to Redcliffe school, I'd come home to Headley Park in the dinner hour, my mother would do egg and chips, or whatever it was, and I would get home in time for Workers' Playtime. You had all the stars of the day. I used to hear a man called Ronnie Ronalde, the world's greatest melodic whistler. I was six, not very clever at school, but I thought "I reckon I can learn to do that". And I did.

Anton: The thing I remember about my childhood is the fun we had of simply making our own pleasures, whether it was a model theatre, or railway layouts, or building castles, and I'm still doing it.

Annie: I save money by making things. This jacket I'm wearing, I couldn't match it, so I bought this curtain material and made these trousers. Who else today would think of doing that?

## There was more sharing then

Don: We weren't rich or anything, but we had most things, and this little boy from down the road would knock on our door and he'd say "Butter". No "please" or anything. A couple of days later he might say "Potatoes". My father was at BAC working away. He would go crackers if he found out.

The reckoning is coming whether we like it or not. We'll be forced back to the old ways, back to sharing. It's from the moment that we're forced that we'll change. The majority want their cars and everything else till the last minute. We're living as individuals, whizzing round the world like billy-o, enjoying ourselves while the world is three quarters starving.

Anton: There will be a catastrophe, a big, big catastrophe.

Sue: I don't know whether we can stop it.

## We can stop it

Heather: Of course we can! It's just putting your mind to it. A lot of these big companies want to keep things the way they are because they don't want change. If you become independent they don't make so much money. But I think we should end our dependency on oil. I think we should be moving towards it now.

I would like to see community power, say a solar panel on every house on our estate, even a small windmill. If you can get a community together and build a system to power the whole estate, that's a big step.

# Were the old times better?

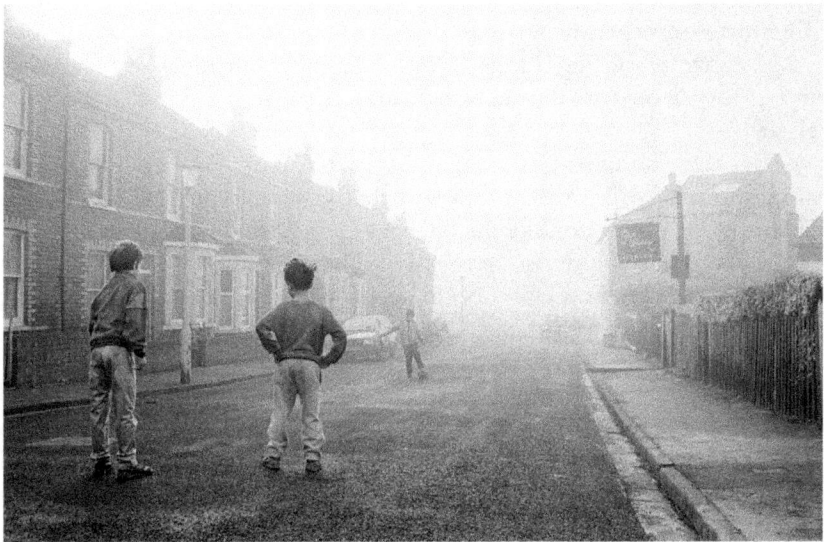

All the people we interviewed have lived lower carbon life-styles. Was it better or worse, and will life feel good where we are headed?

Cheap energy, be it gas, electricity or petrol, has transformed our lives. We travel all over the world and use machines to do the once back-breaking work of washing clothes. New and old technology can help us maintain a good material life without destroying the world we live in, even if some big changes are inevitable. We can choose technologies that significantly improve our lives, like computers and washing machines, while cycle tours across Somerset could replace plane journeys to India and Australia.

Despite all our extra consumption, research suggests that people are no happier now than they were fifty years ago, and there is a higher incidence of stress and mental illness.

Poverty and injustice make people miserable. Another big factor is lack of community – and poverty and injustice contribute to that. But even when things are hard, how happy or miserable people are seems to depend mainly on how they get on together.

In the old days, if you had a sense of belonging, if you were supported by friendly people around you, life could be good even when it was less comfortable than it is now. Organising to make things better for everyone; to build less wasteful, more productive communities could be a way to a happier life for us too.

## The long emergency

Now we are facing a long-term emergency, but most of us are just trying to get on with business as usual, because we don't know what else to do.

We can't wait for governments to act for us. Sooner or later the environmental crisis will get so bad that governments will finally take action, but we may not like the changes they impose.

Many of the solutions – technological and cultural – are already out there. If we start thinking about what needs to happen locally now, we'll be in a strong position to make a better future.

## Transition Bristol

Bristol is part of the transition towns movement. The idea is to strengthen communities across the city, using the skills, knowledge and creativity of ordinary Bristolians, so that together we can face the challenges of climate change and peak oil.

The long term aim is more resilient, happier communities. Bristol needs to leave behind its addiction to cheap fossil fuels and build on the resources in and around the city region.

- Imagine... a Bristol full of fruit trees, with food grown in window boxes, back yards and allotments, cooperative farming within easy reach of Bristol. Community supported agriculture projects like at Chew Magna and Sims Hill help ordinary people co-operate on a bigger scale. We need more people from all backgrounds to join projects like these.
- Imagine central Bristol, with clean air, kids playing safely in the street and people of all ages sharing the public space without fear of fast moving cars.
- Imagine... free practical help for all households to reduce energy consumption, learning from our neighbours – improved insulation, smart meters, solar panels etc.
- Imagine... all Bristol schoolchildren learn to grow food, repair and recycle computers, clothes and bikes, save energy – schools have their own gardens and could reuse old computers.

- Imagine... supermarkets, other shops, corporations and factories obliged to clear up their waste, instead of this expense falling to the local taxpayer.
- Imagine... well organised free community skills swaps, with help for disabled people and others who can't currently swap skills.
- Imagine... more community parties, bringing local food to share, with music, art and dance.
- Imagine... free bikes to borrow to get around the city, free classes to learn safe cycling, car clubs, and far fewer cars on the roads and therefore fewer road traffic accidents.
- Imagine... cheap, reliable, local and inter-city public transport.
- Imagine... Bristol's own currency, money that circulates wealth within community and avoids profiteering banks. (The Bristol Pound is already happening.)
- Imagine... properly resourced communities, where neighbours deal with everyday disputes by mediation and negotiation, with many more community centres welcoming parents with young children and anyone lonely during the day.
- Imagine....

All of these are possible. Some exist already – and you may have other ideas yourself.

www.transitionbristol.org

# Acknowledgements

All photographs by Mark Simmons

Diagrams on pages 9 & 10 by Adam Nieman / Carbon Visuals

Older Women for World Change are grateful to Mark Simmons, Ciaran Mundy and Adam Nieman for their help.

Thanks also to Pat Simmons, Barbara Charnock and Clare Sandler who helped with the interviews and with earlier versions of this booklet, to Ellen Malos for copy-editing, and to all our interviewees.

www.ingramcontent.com/pod-product-compliance
Lightning Source LLC
Chambersburg PA
CBHW071648170526
45166CB00003B/1486